Pontifical Council for
Social Communications

Pastoral Instruction

DAWN

OF A

NEW ERA

On the Twentieth Anniversary of
Communio et Progressio

Aetatis Novae

St. Paul Books & Media

ISBN 0-8198-6949-X

Vatican Translation

Printed and published in the U.S.A. by St. Paul Books & Media, 50 St. Paul's Avenue, Boston, MA 02130

St. Paul Books & Media is the publishing house of the Daughters of St. Paul, an international congregation of women religious serving the Church with the communications media.

1 2 3 4 5 6 7 8 9   99 98 97 96 95 94 93 92

INTRODUCTION

A REVOLUTION IN HUMAN COMMUNICATIONS

1. At the dawn of a new era, a vast expansion of human communications is profoundly influencing culture everywhere. Revolutionary technological changes are only part of what is happening. Nowhere today are people untouched by the impact of media upon religious and moral attitudes, political and social systems, and education.

It is impossible to ignore, for instance, that geographical and political boundaries were both of very little avail in view of the role played by communications during the "radical transformations" of 1989 and 1990, on whose historical significance the Pope reflects in *Centesimus Annus.*[1]

It becomes equally evident that the first "Areopagus of the modern age is the world of communications which is unifying humanity and turning it into what is known as a 'global village.' The means of social communications have become so important as to be for many the chief means of information and education, of guidance and inspiration in their behavior as individuals, families and within society at large."[2]

More than a quarter century after the promulgation of the Second Vatican Council's decree on social communications, *Inter Mirifica,* and two decades after the pastoral instruction *Communio et Progressio,* the Pontifical Council for Social

Communications wishes to reflect on the pastoral implications of this situation.

We do so in the spirit expressed by the closing words of *Communio et Progressio:* "The people of God walk in history. As they...advance with their times, they look forward with confidence and even with enthusiasm to whatever the development of communications in a space age may have to offer."[3]

Taking for granted the continued validity of the principles and insights of these conciliar and post-conciliar documents, we wish to apply them to new and emerging realities. We do not pretend to say the final word on a complex, fluid, rapidly changing situation, but simply wish to provide a working tool and a measure of encouragement to those confronting the pastoral implications of the new realities.

2. In the years since *Inter Mirifica* and *Communio et Progressio* appeared, people have grown accustomed to expressions like *information society, mass-media culture* and *media generation.* Terms like these underline a remarkable fact: Today, much that men and women know and think about life is conditioned by the media; to a considerable extent, human experience itself is an experience of media.

Recent decades also have witnessed remarkable developments in the technology of communicating. These include both the rapid evolution of previously existing technologies and the emergence of new telecommunications and media technologies: satellites, cable television, fiber optics, videocassettes, compact disks, computerized image making and other computer and digital technology, and much else. The use of new media gives rise to what some speak of as "new languages" and has given birth to new possibilities for the mission of the Church as well as to new pastoral problems.

3. Against this background we encourage the pastors and people of the Church to deepen their understanding of issues relating to communications and media, and to translate their

understanding into practical policies and workable programs.

"As the council fathers looked to the future and tried to discern the context in which the Church would be called upon to carry out her mission, they could clearly see that the progress of technology was already 'transforming the face of the earth' and even reaching out to conquer space. They recognized that developments in communications technology, in particular, were likely to set off chain reactions with unforeseen consequences."[4]

"Far from suggesting that the Church should stand aloof or try to isolate herself from the mainstream of these events, the council fathers saw the Church as being in the very midst of human progress, sharing the experiences of the rest of humanity, seeking to understand them and to interpret them in the light of faith. It was for God's faithful people to make creative use of the new discoveries and technologies for the benefit of humanity and the fulfillment of God's plan for the world...employing the full potential of the 'computer age' to serve the human and transcendent vocation of every person, and thus to give glory to the Father from whom all good things come."[5]

We express our gratitude to those responsible for the creative communications work under way in the Church everywhere. Despite difficulties—arising from limited resources, from the obstacles sometimes placed in the way of the Church's access to media and from a constant reshaping of culture, values and attitudes brought about by the pervasive presence of media—much has been and continues to be accomplished. The dedicated bishops, clergy, religious and lay people engaged in this critically important apostolate deserve the thanks of all.

Also welcome are those positive ventures in media-related ecumenical cooperation involving Catholics and their brothers and sisters of other churches and ecclesial communities, as well as interreligious cooperation with those of other world religions. It is not only appropriate but "necessary for Christians to work together more effectively in their communications efforts and to act in more direct cooperation with other religions to ensure a united religious presence in the very heart of mass communications."[6]

I. THE CONTEXT OF SOCIAL COMMUNICATIONS

A. Cultural and Social Context

4. As more than just a technological revolution, today's revolution in social communications involves a fundamental reshaping of the elements by which people comprehend the world about them and verify and express what they comprehend. The constant availability of images and ideas, and their rapid transmission even from continent to continent, have profound consequences, both positive and negative, for the psychological, moral and social development of persons, the structure and functioning of societies, intercultural communications, and the perception and transmission of values, worldviews, ideologies and religious beliefs. The communications revolution affects perceptions even of the Church and has a significant impact on the Church's own structures and modes of functioning.

All this has striking pastoral implications. The media can be used to proclaim the Gospel or to reduce it to silence in human hearts. As media become ever more intertwined with people's daily lives, they influence how people understand the meaning of life itself.

Indeed the power of media extends to defining not only what people will think but even what they will think about. Reality, for many, is what the media recognize as real; what media do not acknowledge seems of little importance. Thus de facto silence can be imposed upon individuals and groups whom the media ignore, and even the voice of the Gospel can be muted, though not entirely stilled, in this way.

It is important therefore that Christians find ways to furnish the missing information to those deprived of it and also to give a voice to the voiceless.

The power of media either to reinforce or override the traditional reference points of religion, culture and family underlines the continued relevance of the council's words: "If the media are to be correctly employed, it is essential that all who use them know the principles of the moral order and apply them faithfully in this domain."[7]

B. Political and Economic Context

5. The economic structures of nations are inextricably linked to contemporary communications systems. National investment in an efficient communications infrastructure is widely regarded as necessary to economic and political development, and the growing cost of such investment has been a major factor leading governments in a number of countries to adopt policies aimed at increasing market competition. For this and other reasons, public telecommunications and broadcasting systems in many instances have been subject to policies of deregulation and privatization.

While public systems can clearly be misused for purposes of ideological and political manipulation, unregulated commercialization and privatization in broadcasting can also have far-reaching consequences. In practice, and often as a matter of public policy, public accountability for the use of the airwaves is devalued. Profit, not service, tends to become the most important measure of success. Profit motives and advertisers' interests exert undue influence on media content: Popularity is preferred over quality, and the lowest common denominator prevails. Advertisers move beyond their legitimate role of identifying genuine needs and responding to them, and, driven by profit motives, strive to create artificial needs and patterns of consumption.

Commercial pressures also operate across national boundaries at the expense of particular peoples and their cultures. Faced with increasing competition and the need to develop new markets, communications firms become ever more "multinational" in character; at the same time, lack of local production capabilities makes some countries increasingly dependent on foreign material. Thus, the products of the popular media of one culture spread into another, often to the detriment of established art forms and media and the values which they embody.

Even so, the solution to problems arising from unregulated commercialization and privatization does not lie in state control of media but in more regulation according to criteria of public service and in greater public accountability. It should be noted in this connection that, although the legal and political frameworks within which media operate in some countries are currently changing strikingly for the better, elsewhere government intervention remains an instrument of oppression and exclusion.

II. THE WORK OF THE MEANS OF SOCIAL COMMUNICATIONS

6. *Communio et Progressio* is rooted in a vision of communication as a way toward communion. For "more than the expression of ideas and the indication of emotion," it declares, communication is "the giving of self in love."[8] In this respect, communication mirrors the Church's own communion and is capable of contributing to it.

Indeed, the communication of truth can have a redemptive power, which comes from the person of Christ. He is God's Word made flesh and the image of the invisible God. In and through him God's own life is communicated to humanity by the Spirit's action. "Since the creation of the world, invisible realities, God's eternal power and divinity have become visible, recognized through the things he has made";[9] and now "the Word has become flesh and made his dwelling among us, and we have seen his glory: the glory of an only Son coming from the Father, filled with enduring love."[10]

Here, in the Word made flesh, God's self-communication is definitive. In Jesus' words and deeds the Word is liberating, redemptive, for all humankind. This loving self-revelation of God, combined with humanity's response of faith, constitutes a profound dialogue.

Human history and all human relationships exist within the framework established by this self-communication of God in Christ. History itself is ordered toward becoming a kind of word of God, and it is part of the human vocation to contribute to bringing this about by living out the ongoing, unlimited communication of God's reconciling love in creative new ways. We are to do this through words of hope and deeds of love, that is, through our very way of life. Thus, communication must lie at the heart of the Church community.

Christ is both the content and the dynamic source of the Church's communications in proclaiming the Gospel. For the Church itself is "Christ's mystical body — the hidden completion of Christ glorified — who 'fills the whole creation.'"[11] As a result we move, within the Church and with the help of the word and the sacraments, toward the hope of that last unity where "God will be all in all."[12]

A. Media at the Service of Persons and Cultures

7. For all the good which they do and are capable of doing, mass media, "which can be such effective instruments of unity and understanding, can also sometimes be the vehicles of a deformed outlook on life, on the family, on religion and on morality — an outlook that does not respect the true dignity and destiny of the human person."[13] It is imperative that media respect and contribute to that integral development of the person which embraces "the cultural, transcendent and religious dimensions of man and society."[14]

One also finds the source of certain individual and social problems in the replacement of human interaction by increased media use and intense attachment to fictitious media characters. Media, after all, cannot take the place of immediate personal contact and interaction among family members and friends. But the solution to this difficulty also may lie largely in the media: through their use in ways — dialogue groups, discussions of films and broadcasts — which stimulate interpersonal communication rather than substituting for it.

B. Media at the Service of Dialogue with the World

8. The Second Vatican Council underlined the awareness of the people of God that they are "truly and intimately linked with mankind and its history."[15] Those who proclaim God's word are obligated to heed and seek to understand the "words" of diverse peoples and cultures in order not only to learn from them but to help them recognize and accept the Word of God.[16] The Church therefore must maintain an active, listening presence in relation to the world — a kind of presence which both nurtures community and supports people in seeking acceptable solutions to personal and social problems.

Moreover, as the Church always must communicate its message in a manner suited to each age and to the cultures of particular nations and peoples, so today it must communicate in and to the emerging media culture.[17] This is a basic condition for responding to a crucial point made by the Second Vatican Council: The emergence of "social, technical and cultural bonds" linking people ever more closely lends "special urgency" to the Church's task of bringing all to "full union with Christ."[18] Considering how important a contribution the media of social communications can make to its efforts to foster this unity, the Church views them as means "devised under God's providence" for the promotion of communication and communion among human beings during their earthly pilgrimage.[19]

Thus, in seeking to enter into dialogue with the modern world, the Church necessarily desires honest and respectful dialogue with those responsible for the communications media. On the Church's side this dialogue involves efforts to understand the media — their purposes, procedures, forms and genres, internal structures and modalities — and to offer support and encouragement to those involved in media work. On the basis of this sympathetic understanding and support, it becomes possible to offer meaningful proposals for removing obstacles to human progress and the proclamation of the Gospel.

Such dialogue therefore requires that the Church be actively concerned with the secular media and especially with the shaping of media policy. Christians have in effect a responsibility to make their voice heard in all the media, and their task is not confined merely to the giving out of Church news. The dialogue also involves support for media artists; it requires the development of an anthropology and a theology of communication — not least so that theology itself may be more communicative, more successful in disclosing Gospel values and applying them to the contemporary realities of the human condition; it requires that Church leaders and pastoral workers respond willingly and prudently to media when requested, while seeking to establish relationships of mutual confidence and respect, based on fundamental common values, with those who are not of our faith.

C. Media at the Service of Human Community and Progress

9. Communications in and by the Church is essentially communication of the Good News of Jesus Christ. It is the proclamation of the Gospel as a prophetic, liberating word to the men and women of our times; it is testimony, in the face of radical secularization, to divine truth and to the transcendent destiny of the human person; it is the witness given in solidarity with all believers against conflict and division, to justice and communion among peoples, nations and cultures.

This understanding of communication on the part of the Church sheds a unique light on social communications and on the role which, in the providential plan of God, the media are intended to play in promoting the integral development of human persons and societies.

D. Media at the Service of Ecclesial Communion

10. Along with all this, it is necessary constantly to recall the importance of the fundamental right of dialogue and information within the Church, as described in *Communio et Progressio*,[20] and to continue to seek effective means, including a responsible use of media of social communications, for realizing and protecting this right. In this connection we also have in mind the affirmations of the Code of Canon Law that, besides showing obedience to the pastors of the Church, the faithful "are at liberty to make known their needs, especially their spiritual needs, and their wishes" to these pastors,[21] and that the faithful, in keeping with their knowledge, competence and position, have "the right, indeed at times the duty," to express to the pastors their views on matters concerning the good of the Church.[22]

Partly this is a matter of maintaining and enhancing the Church's credibility and effectiveness. But more fundamentally, it is one of the ways of realizing in a concrete manner the Church's character as *communio,* rooted in and mirroring the intimate communion of the Trinity. Among the members of the community of persons who make up the Church, there is a radical equality in dignity and mission which arises from baptism and underlies hierarchical structure and diversity of office and function; and this equality necessarily will express itself in an honest and respectful sharing of information and opinions.

It will be well to bear in mind, however, in cases of dissent, that "it is not by seeking to exert the pressure of public opinion that one contributes to the clarification of doctrinal issues and renders service to the truth."[23] In fact, "not all ideas which circulate among the people of God" are to be "simply and purely identified with the 'sense of the faith.'"[24]

Why does the Church insist that people have the right to receive correct information? Why does the Church emphasize its right to proclaim authentic Gospel truth? Why does the Church stress the responsibility of its pastors to communicate the truth and to form the faithful to do the same? It is because the whole understanding of what communication in the Church means is based upon the realization that the Word of God communicates himself.

E. Media at the Service of a New Evangelization

11. Along with traditional means such as witness of life, catechetics, personal contact, popular piety, the liturgy and similar celebrations, the use of media is now essential in evangelization and catechesis. Indeed, "the Church would feel guilty before the Lord if she did not utilize these powerful means that human skill is daily rendering more perfect."[25] The media of social communications can and should be instruments in the Church's program of re-evangelization and new evangelization in the contemporary world. In view of the proven efficacy of the old principle "see, judge, act," the audiovisual aspect of media in evangelization should be given due attention.

But it will also be of great importance in the Church's approach to media and the culture they do so much to shape always to bear in mind that: "It is not enough to use the media simply to spread the Christian message and the Church's authentic teaching. It is also necessary to integrate that message into the 'new culture' created by modern communications...with new languages, new techniques and a new psychology."[26] Today's evangelization ought to well up from the Church's active, sympathetic presence within the world of communications.

III. CURRENT CHALLENGES

A. Need for a Critical Evaluation

12. But even as the Church takes a positive, sympathetic approach to media, seeking to enter into the culture created by modern communications in order to evangelize effectively, it is necessary at the very same time that the Church offer a critical evaluation of mass media and their impact upon culture.

As we have said repeatedly, communications technology is a marvelous expression of human genius, and the media confer innumerable benefits upon society. But as we have also pointed out, the application of communications technology has been a mixed blessing, and its use for good purposes requires sound values and wise choices on the part of individuals, the private sector, governments and society as a whole. The Church does not presume to dictate these decisions and choices, but it does seek to be of help by indicating ethical and moral criteria which are relevant to the process — criteria which are to be found in both human and Christian values.

B. Solidarity and Integral Development

13. As matters stand, mass media at times exacerbate individual and social problems which stand in the way of human solidarity and the integral development of the human person. These obstacles include secularism, consumerism, materialism, dehumanization and lack of concern for the plight of the poor and neglected.[27]

It is against this background that the Church, recognizing the media of social communications as "the privileged way" today for the creation and transmission of culture,[28] acknowledges its own duty to offer formation to communications professionals and to the public so that they will approach media with "a critical sense which is animated by a passion for the truth"; it likewise acknowledges its duty to engage in "a work of defense

of liberty, respect for the dignity of individuals and the elevation
of the authentic culture of peoples which occurs through a firm
and courageous rejection of every form of monopoly and manipulation."[29]

C. Policies and Structures

14. Certain problems in this regard arise specifically from
media policies and structures: for example, the unjust exclusion
of some groups and classes from access to the means of communications, the systematic abridgment of the fundamental right to
information, which is practiced in some places, the widespread
domination of media by economic, social and political elites.

These things are contrary to the principal purposes and
indeed to the very nature of the media, whose proper and essential
social role consists in contributing to the realization of the human
right to information, promoting justice in the pursuit of the
common good and assisting individuals, groups and peoples in
their search for truth. The media carry out these crucial tasks
when they foster the exchange of ideas and information among
all classes and sectors of society and offer to all responsible
voices opportunities to be heard.

D. Defense of the Right to Information and Communications

15. It is not acceptable that the exercise of the freedom of
communication should depend upon wealth, education or political power. The right to communicate is the right of all.

This calls for special national and international efforts, not
only to give those who are poor and less powerful access to the
information which they need for their individual and social
development, but to ensure that they are able to play an effective,
responsible role in deciding media content and determining the
structures and policies of their national institutions of social
communications.

Where legal and political structures foster the domination

of the media by elites, the Church for its part must urge respect for the right to communicate, including its own right of access to media, while at the same time seeking alternative models of communications for its own members and for people at large. The right to communicate is part also of the right to religious freedom, which should not be confined to freedom of worship.

IV. PASTORAL PRIORITIES AND RESPONSES

A. *Defense of Human Cultures*

16. Considering the situation in many places, sensitivity to the rights and interests of individuals may often call for the Church to promote alternative community media. Often, too, for the sake of evangelization and catechesis the Church must take steps to preserve and promote folk media and other traditional forms of expression, recognizing that in particular societies these can be more effective than newer media in spreading the Gospel because they make possible greater personal participation and reach deeper levels of human feeling and motivation.

The overwhelming presence of mass media in the contemporary world by no means detracts from the importance of alternative media which are open to people's involvement and allow them to be active in production and even in designing the process of communications itself. Then, too, grassroots and traditional media not only provide an important forum for local cultural expression but develop competence for active participation in shaping and using mass media.

Similarly, we view with sympathy the desire of many peoples and groups for more just, equitable systems of communications and information which safeguard them against domination and manipulation, whether from abroad or at the hands of their fellow countrymen. This is a concern of developing nations in relation to developed ones, and often, too, it is a concern of minorities within particular nations, both developed and developing. In all cases people ought to be able to participate actively, autonomously and responsibly in the process of communications which in so many ways helps to shape the conditions of their lives.

B. Development and Promotion of the Church's Own Media of Social Communications

17. Along with its other commitments in the area of communications and media, the Church must continue, in spite of the many difficulties involved, to develop, maintain and foster its own specifically Catholic instruments and programs for social communications. These include the Catholic press and Catholic publishing houses, Catholic radio and television, offices for public information and media relations, institutes and programs for training in and about media, media research and Church-related organizations of communications professionals — including especially the international Catholic communications organizations — whose members are knowledgeable and competent collaborators with the episcopal conferences as well as with the bishops individually.

Catholic media work is not simply one more program alongside all the rest of the Church's activities: Social communications have a role to play in every aspect of the Church's mission. Thus, not only should there be a pastoral plan for communications, but communications should be an integral part of every pastoral plan, for it has something to contribute to virtually every other apostolate, ministry and program.

C. Formation of Christian Communicators

18. Education and training in communications should be an integral part of the formation of pastoral workers and priests.[30] There are several distinct elements and aspects to the education and training which are required. For example, in today's world,

so strongly influenced by media, Church personnel require at least a working grasp of the impact which new information technologies and mass media are having upon individuals and society. They must likewise be prepared to minister both to the "information-rich" and to the "information-poor." They need to know how to invite others into dialogue, avoiding a style of communicating which suggests domination, manipulation or personal gain. As for those who will be actively engaged in media work for the Church, they need to acquire professional skills in media along with doctrinal and spiritual formation.

D. Pastoral Care of Communications Personnel

19. Media work involves special psychological pressures and ethical dilemmas. Considering how important a role the media play in forming contemporary culture and shaping the lives of countless individuals and whole societies, it is essential that those professionally involved in secular media and the communications industries approach their responsibilities imbued with high ideals and a commitment to the service of humanity.

The Church has a corresponding responsibility to develop and offer programs of pastoral care which are specifically responsive to the peculiar working conditions and moral challenges facing communications professionals. Typically, pastoral programs of this sort should include ongoing formation which will help these men and women — many of whom sincerely wish to know and do what is ethically and morally right — to integrate moral norms ever more fully into their professional work as well as their private lives.

V. THE NEED FOR PASTORAL PLANNING

A. Responsibilities of Bishops

20. Recognizing the validity, and indeed the urgency, of the claims advanced by communications work, bishops and others

responsible for decisions about allocating the Church's limited human and material resources should assign it an appropriate high priority, taking into account the circumstances of their particular nations, regions and dioceses.

This need may be even greater now than previously, precisely because, to some degree at least, the great contemporary "Areopagus" of mass media has more or less been neglected by the Church up to this time.[31] As the Holy Father remarks: "Generally, preference has been given to other means of preaching the Gospel and of Christian education, while the mass media are left to the initiative of individuals or small groups and enter into pastoral planning only in a secondary way."[32] This situation needs correcting.

B. Urgency of a Pastoral Plan for Social Communications

21. We therefore strongly recommend that dioceses and episcopal conferences or assemblies include a communications component in every pastoral plan. We further recommend that they develop specific pastoral plans for social communications itself, or else review and bring up to date those plans which already exist, in this way fostering the desirable process of periodic re-examination and adaptation. In doing so, bishops should seek the collaboration of professionals in secular media and of the Church's own media-related organizations, including especially the international and national organizations for film, radio-television and the press.

Episcopal conferences in some regions already have been well served by pastoral plans which concretely identify needs and goals and encourage the coordination of efforts. The results of the study, assessment and consultation involved in preparing these documents can and should be shared at all levels in the Church, as useful data for pastoral workers. Practical, realistic plans of this sort also can be adapted to the needs of local churches. They should of course be constantly open to revision and adaptation in light of changing needs.

This document itself concludes with elements of a pastoral plan, which also indicate issues for possible treatment in pastoral letters and episcopal statements at the national and local levels. These elements reflect suggestions received from episcopal conferences and media professionals.

CONCLUSION

22. We affirm once again that the Church "sees these media as 'gifts of God,' which in accordance with his providential design unite men in brotherhood and so help them to cooperate with his plan for their salvation."[33] As the Spirit helped the prophets of old to see the divine plan in the signs of their times, so today the Spirit helps the Church interpret the signs of our times and carry out its prophetic tasks, among which the study, evaluation and right use of communications technology and the media of social communications are now fundamental.

APPENDIX

ELEMENTS OF A PASTORAL PLAN FOR SOCIAL COMMUNICATIONS

23. Media conditions and the opportunities presented to the Church in the field of social communications differ from nation to nation and even from diocese to diocese within the same country. It naturally follows that the Church's approach to media and the cultural environment they help to form will differ from place to place, and that its plans and participation will be tailored to local situations.

Every episcopal conference and diocese should therefore develop an integrated pastoral plan for communications, preferably in consultation with representatives of international and national Catholic communications organizations and with local media professionals. Furthermore, communications ought to be taken into account in formulating and carrying out all other pastoral plans, including those concerning social service, education and evangelization. A number of episcopal conferences and dioceses already have developed such plans in which communications needs are identified, goals are articulated, realistic provision is made for financing, and a variety of communications efforts is coordinated.

The following guidelines are offered as assistance to those formulating such pastoral plans or engaged in reassessing plans which exist.

Guidelines for Designing Pastoral Plans for Social Communications in a Diocese, Episcopal Conference or Patriarchal Assembly

24. A pastoral plan for social communications should include the following elements:

a) The statement of a vision, based on extensive consultation, which identifies communications strategies for all Church ministries and responds to contemporary issues and conditions.

b) An inventory or assessment which describes the media environment in the territory under consideration, including audiences, public and commercial media producers and directors, financial and technical resources, delivery systems, ecumenical and educational resources, and Catholic media organizations and communications personnel, including those of religious communities.

c) A proposed structure for Church-related social communications in support of evangelization, catechesis and education, social service and ecumenical cooperation, and including, as far as possible, public relations, press, radio, television, cinema, cassettes, computer networks, facsimile services and related forms of telecommunications.

d) Media education, with special emphasis on the relationship of media and values.

e) Pastoral outreach to, and dialogue with, media professionals, with particular attention to their faith development and spiritual growth.

f) Means of obtaining and maintaining financial support adequate to the carrying out of the pastoral plan.

Process for Designing a Pastoral Plan for Social Communications

25. The plan should offer guidelines and suggestions helpful to Church communicators in establishing realistic goals and priorities for their work. It is recommended that a planning team including Church personnel and media professionals be involved in this process, whose two phases are: 1. research, and 2. design.

Research Phase

26. The elements of the research phase are needs assessment, information gathering, and an exploration of alternative models of a pastoral plan. It includes an analysis of the internal

communications environment, including the strengths and weaknesses of the Church's current structures and programs for communications as well as the opportunities and challenges these face.

Three types of research will assist in gathering the required information: a needs assessment, a communications audit, and a resource inventory. The first identifies areas of ministry requiring particular attention on the part of the episcopal conference or diocese. The second considers what is now being done — including its effectiveness — so as to identify strengths and weaknesses of existing communications structures and procedures. The third identifies communications resources, technology and personnel available to the Church — including not only the Church's "own" resources but those to which it may have access in the business community, the media industries, and ecumenical settings.

Design Phase

27. After gathering and studying these data, the planning team should identify conference or diocesan communications goals and priorities. This is the beginning of the design phase. The planning team should then proceed to address each of the following issues as it relates to local circumstances.

28. *Education.* Communications issues and mass communications are relevant to every level of pastoral ministry, including education. A pastoral social communications plan should attempt:

a) To offer educational opportunities in communications as essential components of the formation of all persons who are engaged in the work of the Church: seminarians, priests, religious brothers and sisters, and lay leaders.

b) To encourage Catholic schools and universities to offer programs and courses related to the communications needs of the Church and society.

c) To offer courses, workshops and seminars in technology,

management and communication ethics and policy issues for Church communicators, seminarians, religious and clergy.

d) To plan and carry out programs in media education and media literacy for teachers, parents and students.

e) To encourage creative artists and writers accurately to reflect Gospel values as they share their gifts through the written word, legitimate theater, radio, television and film for entertainment and education.

f) To identify new strategies for evangelization and catechesis through the application of communications technology and mass communications.

29. *Spiritual formation and pastoral care.* Lay Catholic professionals and others working in either the Church apostolate of social communications or the secular media often look to the Church for spiritual guidance and pastoral care. A pastoral plan for social communications therefore should seek:

a) To offer opportunities for professional enrichment to lay Catholic and other professional communicators through days of recollection, retreats, seminars and professional support groups.

b) To offer pastoral care which will provide the necessary support, nourish the communicators' faith, and keep alive their sense of dedication in the difficult task of communicating Gospel values and authentic human values to the world.

30. *Cooperation.* Cooperation involves sharing resources among conferences and/or dioceses and between dioceses and other institutions, such as religious communities, universities and health-care facilities. A pastoral plan for social communications should be designed:

a) To enhance relations and encourage mutual consultation between Church representatives and media professionals, who have much to teach the Church about the use of media.

b) To explore cooperative productions through regional and national centers and to encourage the development of joint promotion, marketing and distribution networks.

c) To promote cooperation with religious congregations working in social communications.

d) To collaborate with ecumenical organizations and with other churches and religious groups regarding ways of securing and guaranteeing access to the media by religion, and to collaborate in "the more recently developed media: especially in regard to the common use of satellites, data banks and cable networks, and in informatics generally, beginning with system compatibility."[34]

e) To cooperate with secular media, especially in regard to common concerns on religious, moral, ethical, cultural, educational and social issues.

31. *Public relations.* Public relations by the Church means active communication with the community through both secular and religious media. Involving readiness to communicate Gospel values and to publicize the ministries and programs of the Church, it requires that the Church do all in its power to ensure that its own true image reflects Christ. A pastoral plan for social communications should seek:

a) To maintain public relations offices with adequate human and material resources to make possible effective communication between the Church and the community as a whole.

b) To produce publications and radio, television and video programs of excellent quality which give high visibility to the message of the Gospel and the mission of the Church.

c) To promote media awards and other means of recognition in order to encourage and support media professionals.

d) To celebrate World Communications Day as a means of fostering awareness of the importance of social communications and supporting the communications initiatives of the Church.

32. *Research.* The Church's strategies in the field of social communications must be based on the results of sound media research which have been subjected to informed analysis and evaluation. It is important that communications research include

topics and issues of particular relevance to the mission of the Church in the particular nation and region involved. A pastoral plan for social communications should be designed:

a) To encourage institutes of higher studies, research centers, and universities to engage in both applied and fundamental research related to communications needs and concerns of the Church and society.

b) To identify practical ways of interpreting current communication research and applying it to the mission of the Church.

c) To support ongoing theological reflection upon the processes and instruments of social communication and their role in the Church and society.

33. *Communications and development of peoples.* Accessible point-to-point communication and mass media offer many people a more adequate opportunity to participate in the modern world economy, to experience freedom of expression, and to contribute to the emergence of peace and justice in the world. A pastoral plan for social communications should be designed:

a) To bring Gospel values to bear upon the broad range of contemporary media activities — from book publishing to satellite communications — so as to contribute to the growth of international solidarity.

b) To defend the public interest and to safeguard religious access to the media by taking informed, responsible positions on matters of communications law and policy, and on the development of communications systems.

c) To analyze the social impact of advanced communications technology and to help prevent undue social disruption and cultural destabilization.

d) To assist professional communicators in articulating and observing ethical standards, especially in regard to the issues of fairness, accuracy, justice, decency and respect for life.

e) To develop strategies for encouraging more widespread, representative, responsible access to the media.

f) To exercise a prophetic role by speaking out in timely fashion from a Gospel perspective concerning the moral dimensions of significant public issues.

Vatican City, February 22, 1992, Feast of the Chair of St. Peter the Apostle.

✝ John P. Foley
President
Mons. Pierfranco Pastore
Secretary

NOTES

1. Cf. John Paul II, *Centesimus Annus,* nn. 12-13, in *Acta Apostolicae Sedis,* 1991, pp. 807-821.

2. Ibid., *Redemptoris Missio,* n. 37, in AAS, 1991, p. 285.

3. *Communio et Progressio,* n. 187, in AAS 1971, pp. 655-656.

4. John Paul II, Message for 1990 World Communications Day, *L'Osservatore Romano,* Jan. 25, 1990, p. 6; cf. *Gaudium et Spes,* n. 5.

5. Ibid.

6. Pontifical Council for Social Communications, "Criteria for Ecumenical and Interreligious Cooperation in Communications," n.1, Vatican City, 1989.

7. *Inter Mirifica,* n. 4.

8. *Communio et Progressio,* n. 11.

9. Rom. 1:20.

10. Jn. 1:14.

11. Eph. 3:23; 4:10.

12. 1 Cor. 15:28; *Communio et Progressio,* n. 11.

13. Pontifical Council for Social Communications, "Pornography and Violence in the Media: A Pastoral Response," n. 7, Vatican City, 1989.

14. John Paul II, *Sollicitudo Rei Socialis,* n. 46, in AAS, 1988, p. 579.

15. *Gaudium et Spes,* n. 11.

16. Cf. Paul VI, *Evangelii Nuntiandi,* n. 20, in AAS, 1976, pp. 18-19.

17. Cf. *Inter Mirifica,* n. 3.

18. *Lumen Gentium,* n. 1.

19. Cf. *Communio et Progressio,* n. 12.

20. Ibid., 114-121.

21. Cf. Canon 212.2.

22. Cf. Canon 212.3.

23. Congregation for the Doctrine of the Faith, "Instruction on the Ecclesial Vocation of the Theologian," n. 30, in AAS, 1990, p. 1562.

24. Cf. ibid., n. 35.

25. *Evangelii Nuntiandi,* n. 45.

26. *Redemptoris Missio,* n. 37.

27. *Centesimus Annus,* n. 41.

28. John Paul II, *Christifideles Laici,* in AAS, 1989, p. 480.

29. Ibid., p. 481.

30. Cf. Congregation for Catholic Education, "Guide to the Training of Future Priests Concerning the Instruments of Social Communications," Vatican City, 1986.

31. Cf. *Redemptoris Missio,* n. 37.

32. Ibid.

33. *Communio et Progressio,* n. 2.

34. "Criteria for Ecumenical and Interreligious Cooperation in Communications," n. 14.

St. Paul Book & Media Centers:

ALASKA
750 West 5th Ave., Anchorage, AK 99501 **907-272-8183.**
CALIFORNIA
3908 Sepulveda Blvd., Culver City, CA 90230 **213-397-8676.**
1570 Fifth Ave. (at Cedar Street), San Diego, CA 92101 **619-232-1442;
619-232-1443.**
46 Geary Street, San Francisco, CA 94108 **415-781-5180.**
FLORIDA
145 S.W. 107th Ave., Miami, FL 33174 **305-559-6715; 305-559-6716.**
HAWAII
1143 Bishop Street, Honolulu, HI 96813 **808-521-2731.**
ILLINOIS
172 North Michigan Ave., Chicago, IL 60601 **312-346-4228;
312-346-3240.**
LOUISIANA
4403 Veterans Memorial Blvd., Metairie, LA 70006 **504-887-7631;
504-887-0113.**
MASSACHUSETTS
50 St. Paul's Ave., Jamaica Plain, Boston, MA 02130 **617-522-8911.**
Rte. 1, 885 Providence Hwy., Dedham, MA 02026 **617-326-5385.**
MISSOURI
9804 Watson Rd., St. Louis, MO 63126 **314-965-3512; 314-965-3571.**
NEW JERSEY
561 U.S. Route 1, Wick Plaza, Edison, NJ 08817 **908-572-1200;**
NEW YORK
150 East 52nd Street, New York, NY 10022 **212-754-1110.**
78 Fort Place, Staten Island, NY 10301 **718-447-5071; 718-447-5086.**
OHIO
2105 Ontario Street (at Prospect Ave.), Cleveland, OH 44115
216-621-9427.
PENNSYLVANIA
214 W. DeKalb Pike, King of Prussia, PA 19406 **215-337-1882;
215-337-2077.**
SOUTH CAROLINA
243 King Street, Charleston, SC 29401 **803-577-0175.**
TEXAS
114 Main Plaza, San Antonio, TX 78205 **512-224-8101.**
VIRGINIA
1025 King Street, Alexandria, VA 22314 **703-549-3806.**
CANADA
3022 Dufferin Street, Toronto, Ontario, Canada M6B 3T5 **416-781-9131.**

St. Paul Books & Media